# YOUR KNOWLEDGE H

Pascal Adams

**Fans, the Bundesliga and the Standing Room Debate.
A study of the German Football Stadium Experience**

GRIN Verlag

**Bibliografische Information der Deutschen Nationalbibliothek:**

Die Deutsche Bibliothek verzeichnet diese Publikation in der Deutschen National-
bibliografie; detaillierte bibliografische Daten sind im Internet über http://dnb.d-
nb.de/ abrufbar.

**Imprint:**

Copyright © 2013 GRIN Verlag GmbH
Druck und Bindung: Books on Demand GmbH, Norderstedt Germany
ISBN: 978-3-656-59963-0

**This book at GRIN:**

http://www.grin.com/en/e-book/269436/fans-the-bundesliga-and-the-standing-
room-debate-a-study-of-the-german

**GRIN - Your knowledge has value**

Der GRIN Verlag publiziert seit 1998 wissenschaftliche Arbeiten von Studenten, Hochschullehrern und anderen Akademikern als eBook und gedrucktes Buch. Die Verlagswebsite www.grin.com ist die ideale Plattform zur Veröffentlichung von Hausarbeiten, Abschlussarbeiten, wissenschaftlichen Aufsätzen, Dissertationen und Fachbüchern.

**Visit us on the internet:**

http://www.grin.com/

http://www.facebook.com/grincom

http://www.twitter.com/grin_com

**TITLE PAGE**

Name        Pascal Adams

Degree      MSc Sport and Exercise Management


Title       **FANS, THE BUNDESLIGA AND THE STANDING ROOM**

            **DEBATE: A STUDY OF THE GERMAN FOOTBALL STADIUM**

            **EXPERIENCE**


Presented as Part of the Requirement for the

MSc Sport & Exercise Management at

University College Dublin.

i

# ABSTRACT

This study looks at the current issues surrounding football fan behaviour, more specifically the fan problems in German football stadiums. Removing the standing room areas to curb negative fan behaviour while upholding the fan culture is currently under debate. It is important to research this debate as the outcome will have a major impact on the future success of Germany's beloved football. This research analyses different areas of the fan experience including the dangers of Bengalos in the standing room areas, football and non-football fans' positive and negative opinions of the stadium experience, and possible solutions to protect the image of German Football. Using fan surveys from 100 respondents and analysing the quantitative data gives insight into the respondents' opinions on the standing room's importance as an integral part of the football experience. The results show that the Bundesliga has a successful product on the field and boasts a fan friendly environment which makes it a unique League in Europe. The consensus among the respondents is to protect this culture and find a sustainable solution to the stadium disturbances, which fits into the business model of the Bundesliga.

# CONTENTS

# LIST OF TABLES

# LIST OF FIGURES

# CHAPTER 1

# INTRODUCTION

## 1.1 Introduction

An increasing number of incidents of aggressive behaviour among football fans have the German Football League, (DFL), the clubs and the German Football Federation, (DFB) worried. Politicians and the German government are now getting involved due to escalating cases and more tax money spent on policing the games. It is estimated that it costs around €100 million per season for police presence at football games (Schöbel 2011). The football clubs are coming together to try and improve the safety regulations despite opposition from some fans (John and Luetticke 2012). The problems occur not only in the stadium but also on arrival to and departure from the stadiums. According to an interview with Interior Minister Pistorius, around 16,500 people were responsible for violence in the 2011/2012 season (Bewarder and Lutz 2013). The government official explains that 787 people were injured during the season of which 242 were police officers. Another article reports how the football club HSV, in Hamburg had to pay 100,000€ in penalties due to their fans' behaviour in home and away games (Pegelow 2012). Another harrowing account describes how a busload of Mönchengladbach supporters were attacked by Cologne supporters and forced off the freeway and then attacking the bus with baseball bats, iron rods and bricks causing €26,000 in damage (Wallrodt 2012).

Fan behaviour is not only an issue in Germany but also in other leagues around the world. "Ultras" or hard-core fan groups sometimes throw flares or Bengalos onto the

1

pitch, into the stands or hold the flares in a packed surrounding (Ruf 2012). They are coordinated in their actions, testing the limits and public safety. Some of these groups are linked to hooliganism and racism and concerns are growing. Due to the increased number of incidents, the DFB in addition to politicians and the government have suggested changes since the talks with these fans have not come to any sustainable solution.

This study investigates current problems in German stadiums, possible solutions to the problems and the resulting impact on fan culture, and offers recommendations for next steps forward in order to preserve the special relationship between German football fans and their clubs.

## 1.2 The Bundesliga

The Bundesliga, or German Football League, consists of the top division and the second division. It is quickly becoming one of the top leagues in the world with efficient discretionary spending, providing a top quality product on the field (Conn 2013). Due to the recent success in the Champions League, there has been more attention paid to the league. Two German teams, Borussia Dortmund and Bayern Munich, played in the Champions League final on 26 May, 2013 in London which has created some added exposure for the Bundesliga and its business approach. The financial aspect plays a large role as strict attention is paid to the amount of money being spent and earned. This is in line with the UEFA Financial Fair Play regulations which restrict club spending to sixty per cent of their turnover (Herbert 2012). Currently, fourteen of the eighteen clubs in the first division of the Bundesliga are currently recording a profit (ESPN 2013).

2

The clubs in the Bundesliga, both the first and second division, are not owned by foreign investors as is the case in the English Premier League. German clubs are owned by their members and are governed by a rule that members have to have a majority vote of 51 shares in all decision making processes (Conn 2012). Journalist David Conn explains that this rule allows the clubs to have deep roots in their communities and nurtures the grassroots development of players rather than being a club funded by wealthy individuals. This system seems to be working well for the Bundesliga as in their fiftieth season the revenue of the League has surpassed two billion euros for the first time (dr/jr 2013). According to the article, the Bundesliga also has the highest attendance record in the world with second place going to the English Premier League.

### 1.3 Fan Culture

The Bundesliga teams pride themselves on offering a fan friendly environment by keeping the ticket prices low and encouraging a fan and terrace culture in their stadiums. Not only are the fans members of the organization but the clubs encourage the fans with these initiatives to fill the stadium. There is a feeling among the fans that they are participants in the actual organization rather than bystanders (Liew 2013). Their voice is heard, appreciated and valued by each of the clubs.

### 1.4 Ticketing Philosophy

Each of the stadiums in the first and second division of the Bundesliga offer a large section of standing room only areas. As the journalist Conn writes in his article, the fans who make up the famous "yellow wall", which is the standing area in Dortmund's

3

stadium, can buy tickets for as cheap as eleven euros (2012). Every team in the league has this philosophy of giving back to the fans.

Even the team which has the most money, Bayern Munich, has the same fan friendly policies. The president of the team, Uli Hoeness, recently explained his thought process behind the decision on ticket pricing. A season ticket in the standing areas can be purchased for as little as €120 (Shergold 2013). Shergold explains that the cheapest season ticket in the English Premier League, for Wigan, which was recently relegated to the second division, sells for close to €300. Hoeness rejects charging a larger amount for tickets as it would not create any significant difference for the club's revenue stream while it would make a dent in the fans' disposable income, "We do not think the fans are like cows, who you milk. Football has got to be for everybody"(Shergold 2013).

## 1.5 Pyrotechnics

Although the German Football League and the clubs have an inclusive and appreciative stance towards fans, there is a growing threat to this philosophy. There has been an increased use of pyrotechnics in the stadiums in Germany. Pyrotechnics are fireworks that are ignited by lighting the magnesium. They produce light effects and a lot of smoke (Zeus 2013). The fans use pyrotechnics called 'bengalisches Feuer' or Bengalos which is a type of flare. Fans smuggle them into the stadium as they are illegal. Since the flares can be as small as a lipstick, they are hard to detect by security personnel; women can smuggle them in easily (Fritz 2012).

Bengalos are normally used on boats for rescue missions on oceans or seas. Once the Bengalo is ignited, it cannot be extinguished by either sand or water and can burn at over 1000 degrees Centigrade even when the flame has finished burning (RPO 2012). This is what makes the flare so dangerous in an enclosed space with thousands of people in the immediate surroundings. Officials are worried because of fire safety issues and even the possibility of death in an area filled with people and no quick way to escape. In addition, the smoke from setting off the flare can cause an added health hazard when inhaling it. Fans sometimes use the smoke coming from these pyrotechnics to storm the field of play before the match is even over (Fritz 2012).

## 1.6 European Leagues

The Bundesliga is not the only League that is facing issues as other Leagues around the world and specifically in Europe are dealing with issues relating to fan behaviour and racism. The English Premier League and the Italian League is dealing with racist incidents on almost a weekly basis. UEFA, the governing body of European football has taken a stronger stance against fan behaviour issues especially racism. They are implementing a 10 match ban for any racist abuse on the field while threatening to close part of the stadium should abuse come from the fan sections (McGowan 2013).

## 1.7 This study

This study examines the German Football League's history and its growth, its fan culture and potential, and how problems in fan behaviour can affect the German Football League's future. Through a survey the study will determine both football and non-football fans' views of the current stadium experience. Are fans aware of problems in the stadium, in particular in reference to the use of pyrotechnics, as reported in the media? Are fans aware of the controversial debate on removing the popular standing room areas due to negative fan behaviour and what impact will this have on the stadium experience? Do fans think that change is necessary in the stadiums to protect the safety of the spectators? And finally, if change is necessary for stronger control of fan behaviour, what is the best method to bring about a change which will be accepted by all to sustain the success of the German Football League? The study will address these questions and, based on survey results as well as current literature, offer recommendations for an approach to solving some of the negative fan atmosphere issues currently escalating in Germany.

## 1.8 Justification

This study is relevant and important because of the attention this topic has received both in the media and among government agencies in Germany. It is current because the decisions to be made on the elimination of the standing room areas in German football stadiums could have an impact on the future of the league. Football is a national past time in Germany and all parties affected are working to find a viable solution. The study is particularly interesting to the author because he is from Germany and has been following developments in these related areas of sports governance, business, racism and fan behaviour.

# CHAPTER 2

## LITERATURE REVIEW

### 2.1 Introduction

Using the literature available on this topic, this chapter will give some background information on football in Germany and its history, the financial aspect of the game in Europe as well as fan behaviour and racism. This will allow the reader to understand the changes the sport has gone through and how some of the decisions, especially concerning fan issues are made today. Understanding this history as discussed in current literature is important when looking at the survey results and the resulting discussion of fan behaviour in German football stadiums.

### 2.2 Football in Europe

Football in Europe is growing into a big business. Money is being spent in order for the clubs and the owners to win illustrious national and European titles. In the UK most of the clubs are owned by billionaires, and this has crossed over into some of the other Leagues as well, for example, in France. Martin describes that in 12 years in the Bundesliga there was an increase in turnover of 75 million Deutsch Mark (2005). Frick outlines the increase in the average player's salary from €550k in 1996 to over €1million in 2006 in the Bundesliga (2007). Martin points out that international competition has not only increased earnings but has also broadcast images of the different European Leagues across borders, making the European Leagues more international. This spread of the game has led to an increase in movement from fans who travel all over Europe to support their team (King 2000).

This movement of players among different European Leagues was first made possible by the Bosman ruling as Frick recognized (2009). He describes this progress as initiated by a Belgian footballer in 1995, Jean-Marc-Bosman, who sued his old club because of a restriction on trade. Bosman won the case based on violation of his rights of freedom to move for labour. This changed the movement of players because the restrictions for foreigners to play for a club were lifted (Frick 2009). This has definitely affected the number of local players for a club from the same country; however, the movement across borders cannot be linked solely to the Bosman ruling but can be attributed to the change in society and the change in European football in general. This is especially interesting when looking at fans' racist reactions because the globalization of the Leagues should be a defining factor in subduing racist behaviour.

The movement of players and the revenues earned are not the only areas which have changed in football. This has had an impact on the way the clubs are governed as indicated by Holt (2007). Holt points out that the commercialization of the sport and the Bosman ruling has increased the power stakeholders have gained because of the need to protect their investments. As Holt explains, everyone from the elite clubs to the national associations and the government have different interests in the football competitions with a majority of these interests based on economics.

### 2.3 Football Fans

The survey in this research focuses on fan behaviour; therefore it is important to examine the fans' involvement in the sport. Merkel praises the German football League for showing its appreciation to its fans through reasonable ticket prices in addition to preserving a standing room culture (2012). He states that in the Bundesliga the fans and the clubs have a friendly relationship which was not always the case. The clubs learned the hard way in relation to TV viewership when it tried to change the broadcasting times and scheduling of the games to try to get fans to pay for the pay TV station Premiere. The fan communities showed their strength in numbers when they abandoned these changes and made the League and TV station regret their decision.

Through fan groups and fan liaison officers, the Bundesliga has developed into a fan friendly League (Merkel 2012). Merkel reiterates this idea in another paper and describes how clubs have tickets geared toward special sectors of society such as students and pensioners (Merkel 2007). Fan culture started off by copying some of the English songs and later looked to the Italian Ultras to form their own Ultra groups.

Brown and Walsh report that fans used to come together to fight against the modernization and commercialization of the game (2000). They outline how fandom is in some cases more than just supporting a club and involves political agendas. Most of the fan groups have been fighting against the commercialization of modern football but in Germany the associations have been working hard to not alienate the fans through this change to a profit-making sport. The German Football Federation has tried to keep the club structure more traditional to protect the fans' interest. This shows how involved and respected fans are amongst the clubs which makes the whole debate that much more interesting because the League has to be careful not to disgruntle these loyal fans.

In the UK, supporters have had different roles such as raising money to keep local clubs alive by trying to go against the modernization of football (Nash 2001).

However, they were not able to go up against the powerful stakeholders and prevent the change in club structure. Some of the problems the fans in the UK came across were the change in demographic of the customers due to the rise in ticket prices. As Nash explains, a reason for this was the behaviour of the fans and the tendency to hooliganism of British supporters.

## 2.4 Football rivalries

While football fans are integral to the experience and atmosphere in the stadium, there are instances when their behaviour goes beyond the sport. This is especially true for football rivalries between football clubs. The meaning of the match gets overblown and spills over into the stands where it becomes a serious matter and can lead to hooliganism. Benkwitz and Molnar note how these fan rivalries create new communities which can affect the surrounding environment (2012). Rivalries can be positive however, the majority of the time it comes with a negative impact and ends in conflict, particular when fans react with racist insult (Benkwitz and Molnar 2012). This conflict stems from the difference in geographical background and has become increasingly apparent when looking at international fixtures. Fans use the different backgrounds of opponents to insult and discriminate against them despite football being a sport that does not discriminate based on race, religion or origin (1995). As Evans and Rowe explain, these issues arise largely due to nationalism (2002).

## 2.5 Ultras

Ultra fan groups have become an increasing problem in German football. They are seen as the main culprits behind the current fan problems; they have, however, existed for a long time in Germany as well as in other Leagues. The German fans first adapted the concept from the Italian Ultra groups (Merkel 2007). In Italy the Ultras developed as a fan culture defined by their geographical location and the bitterness which certain regions feel towards each other (Kassimeris 2011). Kassimeris explains how these groups were spurred on by racism either towards different parts of Italy or people of different races. This racism comes from the history of Italian politics as well as from the fear of migration, and it was present in fan terraces in the stadiums at almost every match especially in the Italian North. Kassiermis notes how Ultras, while mostly right wing, could also have a left wing persuasion which is how they first started in Germany (Merkel 2007).

Ultra's fan activity and hooliganism usually has a cultural and historical background according to Spaaij and Viñas (2005). Although the Ultra movement started in Italy, fans in other countries have adapted it including in Spain. The Spanish fans combined the Italian Ultra concept with English hooliganism to form their own movement. The movement in Spain went beyond the stadium and the club and became a way of life. Although hooligans are more prone to violence and ultras more interested in creating an atmosphere, the ultra-movement in Spain became strongly linked to right wing behaviour. Spaaij and Viñas note that this behaviour always appears in the terraces and that it is linked to social and national identity.

While the predominant Leagues in Europe are in the UK, Italy, Germany and Spain, this negative fan behaviour has spread into other Leagues such as those in the Netherlands. According to Spaaij, hooliganism in the Netherlands has developed from the culture in the UK (2007). He explains how this culture started in terraces where the

11

low cost tickets were sold. The Dutch League removed all standing areas and implemented tighter security. However, the problem still exists since the hooligan groups take their violence outside of the stadium. While the sanctions forced the hooligans to change their ways, they have certainly not disappeared. In this instance removing standing room only moved the problems outside of the stadium which can certainly happen in Germany. This section gives a background of Ultras and their history which will be helpful when examining the reports of fan problems with Ultra groups in Germany.

## 2.6 Football disasters

Looking at fans and stadiums, it is certainly important to examine the safety of the fans. Throughout the years there have been incidents during football matches which have caused a change in regulation. These were not necessarily inflicted through hooliganism or the ultra-movement but rather the inability to cope with crowds. One of those incidents was the Hillsborough disaster in 1989 where ninety-six people died (Scraton 2004). The security stewards, police and emergency services were not able to handle the situation which led to the deaths which was later blamed on the fans. The people were crushed because of poor planning and movement inside and outside of the stadium.

Parties responsible for organization of football matches and regulation were more interested in the match than in the safety of the spectators. Although the stadium might have been filled, people still tried to enter the stadium at any cost (Johnes 2004). Johnes explains that one club removed fire extinguishers from the grounds because they were worried they would be used by hooligans. The stadium actually caught fire and

12

fifty-six people were killed during the match. The UK government had a perception that fans were hooligans and that it was more important to control them rather than to worry about crowd safety (Johnes 2004).

Another incident occurred in 1971 in Glasgow at Ibrox Stadium where 66 people died and 145 were injured because the terraces collapsed under the weight of the crowds (Walker 2004). The feeling of getting crushed in crowds during football matches was normal. Walker explains how after this incident a new act was imposed to control crowd safety. After all of the events, legislation was reviewed and renewed based on the knowledge from each disaster. While these incidents were not a direct result of fan behaviour but rather poor planning and negligence, these articles give an overview of what can happen when many people are in a small space. These articles also describe how regulations were written after the fact, which is something to consider when looking at today's fan behaviour issue and a need to deal with the issue at hand.

**2.7 Racism in German Football**

Football in Germany was underfunded and went through many changes not only during the post WWII Era but also during the Nazi Regime (Kassimeris 2009). The German Football League or Bundesliga did not form until 1963. Politicians and local authorities used the sport to promote their own nationalistic views which at times were racist in nature. Kassimeris explains how even in the 1990's after the reunification of Germany there was a development to expel Jewish people from football and how some teams had supporters who were strongly linked to the old Nazi regime. This was related to the division of the country despite the effort to eliminate racism in sports.

13

Kassimeris reports that racism in German football increased especially after the reintegration of East and West despite there being a number of foreign players after the start of the Bundesliga in 1963 (2009). Racist behaviour was especially present in the lower Leagues of German football.

Kassimeris indicates that this problem spilled over to the World Cup in 2006 although there were no major incidents during the tournament (Kassimeris 2009). The organizational committee tried to immediately squash any type of racist activity before and during the event. He clearly illustrates that the problem of racism in German football stemmed from the early Nazi Regime to the division of East and West and the divide in cultural and social background between the two parts of Germany. This is interesting as it relates to how fan behaviour has been described in the media and how some of the Ultra groups are being linked to right wing aggression. This is an indication of where the problem originates and how far back the issue of racism in Germany goes.

## 2.8 Structure and Financial Analysis of German Football League

The financial situation in football is an important issue since clubs spend millions and accrue large debt. Lago et al. look at this subject closely and analyse the financial situation across the Leagues in Europe (2006). This article is interesting since Lago et al. looked at the situation in 2004 but nothing was done to curb the mounting debt and enormous spending.

Only now UEFA has introduced an agreement to counteract these actions which was already discussed by the governing body in 2004 (Lago et al. 2006). There are three areas which lead to these financial problems. These are loose government regulation, poor club structure and the backing of the government of some teams which can cause difficulties for the government itself in the long run.

Frick and Prinz explain that the Bundesliga teams generate their revenue from TV rights, merchandising and sponsorship and that players in Germany are not paid as much as in other Leagues (2006). They explain that commercialization, tight licensing procedures, and financial controls are the main factors contributing to the success of the Bundesliga. The Bundesliga is unable to match the other leagues in TV money so it has to ensure that its business proceedings are efficiently managed. This section gives an overview of how the revenue of the Bundesliga is generated and the objectives the Bundesliga fulfils under financial fair play guidelines to have a sustainable model for continuous improvement.

To understand the financial model under which the clubs in the Bundesliga operate gives an opportunity to look at their membership model and structure to gain a better overall picture. In spite of being a business, it is less of a hierarchy and more of a democracy when it comes to the decision making process as Wilkesmann and Blutner explain (2002). While clubs in the English Premier League, for example, are predominantly owned by private people who are bankrolling the club's investment, German clubs are made up of members who are part of the association with few exceptions.

Dietl and Franck identify the 50+1 rule as the structure of the club in Germany (2007). The clubs have to hold 50 plus one votes in the club to protect the sport and to avoid any one person buying and controlling the entire team. Even if one person buys up the remaining shares, the control is still with the club or association and its members. This is one of the main reasons why there is a large difference between the leagues in terms of discretionary spending because of the non-existence of private investors financing the clubs.

The involvement of the clubs' members in the decision making process can cause problems as there is an organizational issue accommodating everyone's wishes. It can therefore be harder to focus on the goals and the process of achieving them (Wilkesmann and Blutner 2002). However, German football clubs continue to use this inclusive approach of involving members and officials to try to reach a common goal. These articles emphasize fan involvement rather than exclusion.

## 2.9 Conclusion

This literature review has given background information on the history of football in Germany and described the structure of the game in Europe. In addition, it looked at fan behaviour, racism and Ultra fan groups and their motives as well as the problems that can occur in a stadium when problems escalate. This information will be helpful when looking at the results of the survey research from the standpoint of both football and non-football fans. Comparing the survey results to the information in this review will give an interesting perspective on the issues currently faced in the German Football League.

# CHAPTER 3

## RESEARCH METHODOLOGY

### 3.1 Research Protocol

This study researches the fan atmosphere in German football stadiums. It looks at the perception and feeling among the public while taking into consideration each of the participant's relationship to the game. It also investigates the awareness of the participants of the discussions in the media between the Bundesliga, the fans and the government on the problems which each of these entities believes exist or do not exist. Finally, the study looks at whether a change needs to be implemented in the stadiums and what the solution, if any, should be.

Quantitative research methods were used for this study on fan atmosphere in the stadiums and the issues around this current topic. In order to collect the information about this topic, online surveys were used and distributed. Other types of quantitative research, such as paper surveys, were considered. However, for this study online surveys proved to be beneficial in collecting the data in a short time period. Van Selm and Jankowski explain that online surveys are a useful tool in reaching a broad number of participants in a short amount of time while being cost effective (2006).

Looking at an efficient way to research and portray the type of data required for this research, qualitative research was considered. Using data collection techniques such as interviews would not have been efficient due to the time constraints and the small sample size in relation to surveys. It would have not given representative information on the perception of the population. In addition, quantitative analysis allows the results to be depicted in a clear and concise manner. As Elliott and Williams note, using quantitative analysis can help in portraying a large amount of random results in a simple number form while protecting the identity of the participants (2001).

By using the internet it helped ensure a random population sample across a wide reach of both football fans and non-football fans and of all ages. The survey was written in German because the target demographic was people who spoke German and were living in Germany. This is another reason why online surveys were used because of the geographical differences. According to Theuri and Turner, using the internet for surveys can eliminate any issues that come with constraints due to geography (2002). Since the questions focused on events happening in German football stadiums, it was important that participants from the German population were reached. Subsequently, all the answers were also in German which were translated into English for analysis of this study. The author translated the questions as well as the answers of the open ended questions as he is fluent in both English and German.

## 3.2 Survey Distribution

The survey was setup as anonymous and no personal information was requested during the answering of the questions. The survey was conducted during May and June, 2013 and it was conducted over a three week period of time. The participants had to be over the age of 18 in order to be able to fill out the entire survey. If they were under 18, the survey was terminated to avoid any ethical implications. The link for the survey was sent out using various methods such as emails, public forums and Facebook. The participants were also encouraged to forward the survey to their contacts in order to spread the word, reach a broader audience and increase the sample size.

## 3.3 Data Collection

The survey was made up of 23 questions and split into four sections which were split up by four different pages (see Appendix A). A translated version of the survey in English can be found in Appendix B. Entering the survey; the participants were shown an information sheet which can be found in Appendix C in German and Appendix D in English. This provided relevant information about the study and gave participants the opportunity to contact the author for any further questions. The survey was constructed with a mixture between multiple choice and open ended questions and took about five minutes to complete. A blend was chosen as too many open ended questions, especially in a row, can discourage participants from continuing with the rest of the survey (Granello and Wheaton 2004). All of the multiple choice questions were mandatory, and of the twenty three questions, five questions were open ended of which two were mandatory. While the multiple choice questions offered two to five choices depending on the type of question, the open ended questions all had a text box which allowed the users to write as much as they wished. This way the respondents could voice their opinion on the issue and provide some valuable personal insights.

Each of the pages had a progress bar at the top of the page to indicate how far along the participants were in the survey and how much there was still to fill out. They were also given the opportunity to start the survey and complete it at a later time if they wished to do so. The website umfrageonline.com provided each of the responders with a code which they could enter at their choosing to finish the survey. Using online surveys gives the participants the option of delaying completion of the survey to a more convenient time and making it easy to use (Evans and Mathur 2005).

The first section dealt with areas such as gender, age, whether the respondent was a football fan or not and how often they attended a football game in a stadium. In addition they were also asked how often they watch football in a season. The second section concerned the respondents' preferences and where they like to watch football, in the stadium, with friends, from home or in a bar or restaurant. There were also two open ended questions giving the participant the opportunity to explain their preferences. This gives an idea about the respondent and whether any pattern emerges when looking at the answers of the subsequent questions.

The third section focuses on the debate between football fans and the German Football League, the use of pyrotechnics in the stadiums, the fans' feeling of safety in the arena and participants' opinion on the fan behaviour in the stadiums. The final section dealt with the participants' view on the DFB's idea to eliminate the standing room terraces. The questions asked were whether their view and attendance would change if the standing areas were removed, who is responsible to find a solution and whether getting rid of standing room would be a possible solution as suggested by the DFB. Finally, an open ended question closed the survey to find out how the participants felt about the whole debate between the different parties and their opinion on the best solution.

**3.4 Ethics Exemption**

University College Dublin Ethics Committee issued ethics clearance at the end of April, 2013 after which the online survey was constructed. The Research Ethics Exemption Reference Number was LS-E-13-92-Adams-Matthews. Prior ethics exemption had been approved. However, due to the change in research from a media and desk based study to online surveys, new ethics approval had to be granted. Due to the fact that no vulnerable groups were used in this research and that all participants had to be over the age of 18, the University College Dublin Ethics Committee issued approval. In addition to the ethics application, an information sheet was attached which the contributors were able to read as soon as they entered the link for the survey. Since all the answers were anonymous and no personal data was saved during the completion of the survey, no consent form had to be issued.

**3.5 Test Session**

Prior to sending the surveys out to the general population, a test survey was sent out to ten participants, both football and non-football fans in order to make sure the survey was understandable and the results answered the questions necessary for this research. Testing the survey before the final product is sent out is absolutely vital when using surveys for research (Hunt et al. 1982). After making a few changes, adding several open ended questions and going over the survey with the supervisor, Dr. Tara Magdalinski, the survey was finalised and ready to be distributed in May, 2013.

## 3.6 Data Analysis

The results from the 100 participants were evaluated using different methods. The survey tool used to gather the information and conduct surveys is from the website umfrageonline.com. The website allowed for basic analysis of all the answers, portraying the answers in a pie diagram as well as percentages. In addition to using the resources available through the website, Microsoft Excel 2010 was used to conduct further analysis of the answers. The data from the website was downloaded to an excel spread sheet which was helpful when comparing different statistics to each other and representing them either in a graph or in table. IBM SPSS 20 was used to portray these graphs. The excel spread sheets together with the statistics software gave the opportunity to illustrate the results in tables and graphs to produce the results which are presented in this study. These tools were used only for the multiple choice questions and answers while the open ended answers were examined and analysed throughout the results and discussion chapter.

The data collected by using this research method will be described in the next chapter.

# CHAPTER 4

# RESULTS AND DISCUSSION

## 4.1 Introduction

The results of the survey on fan atmosphere are presented in this chapter. The four different sections of the survey are analysed which are demographics of participants, preferences, the respondents' views on fan behaviour and the suggested solutions. The results are discussed and the main themes from the open ended questions presented.

## 4.2 Background information on Participants

The first section of the survey dealt with the profile of the respondents to the survey. After analysing the 100 responses, 77 per cent of the responses came from male participants and 23 per cent from female participants. Only seven per cent of respondents were members of fan clubs in Germany.

Most respondents (44%) were between the ages of 25 and 35, seventeen per cent between eighteen and 24, while 21 per cent were between 35 and fifty, and 18 per cent over the age of fifty. The average age range of the respondents was 25 to 35. This will give good information on how the different age groups feel about fan atmosphere in Germany. Of all the respondents, seventy per cent were football fans, five per cent were non-football fans and 25 per cent were casual fans who do not consider themselves a football fan but do enjoy following the occasional game. Out of the 23 per cent of female respondents, ten per cent were also football fans and thirteen per cent were occasional fans. None of the female respondents considered themselves non-football fans.

Figure 4.1 below shows the percentage of respondents who watched a given number of games in a season. Each team plays 34 games in a season in the first division of the Bundesliga. Out of the respondents who watched twenty or more games, five per cent were female football fans. Thus it is predominantly male football fans who watch the most games in a season.

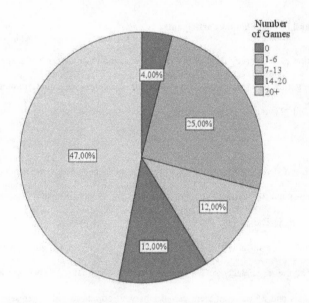

**Figure 4.1 Percentage of respondents who watched a given number of games in a season**

Table 4.1 gives an overview of how often respondents went to a game in a stadium. Forty per cent who attended between zero and four games in a stadium were between the ages of eighteen and 35. The ten per cent who attended seventeen or more games in a stadium also watched twenty or more games in a season, were all male and five per cent were members of fan clubs. Since each team plays seventeen home and seventeen away games, this means that these ten per cent also travelled across Germany to follow their team. The survey shows that most attendants at stadium games are young males between the ages of eighteen and 35.

**Table 4.1 The number of times respondents attended games in a stadium during a season**

| Number of Games | 0 | 1-4 | 5-10 | 11-17 | 17+ |
|---|---|---|---|---|---|
| Number of attendances | 35 | 41 | 9 | 5 | 10 |

### 4.3 Participants' preferences

The football experience in a stadium should be something that can be enjoyed by many people of different ages. Nelson Mandela explains that sport "has the power to unite people" (Hughes 2013) and therefore an experience in a stadium should be a fun event for everyone including families. Most respondents (76%) believe that a stadium experience can be enjoyed with their family, children and grandchildren. Only twenty four per cent say that they would not attend with their family. From the survey it appears that most are not deterred by fan behaviour and dangers of pyrotechnics. This could be related to the fact that each stadium in the Bundesliga has a family section and special pricing for tickets which makes it attractive for families to attend the games (Dobbert 2012).

When researching how respondents preferred to enjoy the games in the stadium, most (58%) preferred to sit, while 23 per cent would rather stand and nineteen per cent would choose either standing or sitting. The preferred place to watch the games was the stadium rather than anywhere else, though 26 per cent preferred to watch the game in a bar or restaurant. While 24 per cent would rather watch football in their own home, fourteen per cent indicated they would prefer to watch at a friend's house.

There are several reasons why participants chose their answers to these two questions. Some of them relate to personal preference but some also relate to safety and concerns about fan atmosphere. Respondents answered that they thought it is more comfortable and relaxing to sit down for the duration of the game. Sitting down is also safer, and one can observe the mood in the stadium rather than being right in the middle of the action. One person also thinks that "the sitting areas are occupied by the older generation, and are more peaceful and there are no riots". Some also suggest that it depends on who they go with. If they are in the stadium with their friends, they would rather stand because the atmosphere is better; however, seven per cent mentioned that if they are attending the game with family, they would rather sit as the standing areas are no place for children.

Researching why people would chose to stand in the standing areas, fourteen per cent believe the atmosphere in the standing room is where the excitement originates and that this area is unmatched anywhere else in the stadium. This is the only way to truly support their team. Respondents think one should move, be active and show emotions since it is a sporting event and not a theatre production. According to the survey, it is a completely different experience when standing, to feel the excitement of the fans. One fan reports, "In the standing areas I can witness and create the atmosphere, and it gives me a sense of freedom."

Safety in the standing room is a concern for sixteen per cent and that is why they choose to sit. The respondents are worried about the culture in standing room areas, "hooligans are present in the standing areas", and about the tight spaces to stand in. The pushing and shoving in these areas deters people from standing. According to 43 per cent who chose sitting over standing, they did so because it is a more convenient way to watch the game. There is also the issue of seeing the field which is more problematic when standing and therefore some respondents decide to sit because of the unobstructed view.

Safety was also an issue in selecting game viewing options. Outside of the stadium they identified as being the safer option. The respondents thought that due to a smaller number of people and no major arrival and departure procedure under police supervision, there were fewer chances of unsafe incidents. As one fan explains "there are too many people in the stadium and one does not know if safety is guaranteed."

In the stadium there is a different "vibe", which is why survey participants chose to go to the stadium, because of this unique atmosphere. The feeling of being in the stadium, right there in the midst of the action could not be repeated anywhere else. Out of the 76 per cent who answered this question, 38 per cent mentioned that the atmosphere was their main reason why they would go to the stadium. The respondents thought that when watching the games on TV, one is dependent on what the broadcasters show on the screen, while in the stadium one can see the entire field and get a sense of the mood amongst the supporters. There is also a sense of camaraderie among the spectators when they are together in the stadium cheering on their team; the respondents see the event in the stadium as a social event. Attending the game in the stadium makes it an active experience, while sitting at home is more passive. One fan referred to the stadium experience as "reality football."

While the stadium experience is fun, exciting and energizing some respondents prefer to unwind and not have to deal with the crowds at the stadium. As the survey suggests, the main reason respondents gave for preferring to watch the game either at home or at a friend's house was comfort. Watching from home or in a restaurant or bar was a more convenient choice for fifteen per cent of the respondents. One fan even makes his choice to watch alone based on superstition, believing that "my team always loses if I decide to watch the game with my friends." Another factor which discouraged respondents from going to the stadium was price. The tickets for the standing room, which are the cheapest ticket in the stadium, are usually sold out fairly quickly and prices for seats are higher. According to eight per cent of the respondents, tickets were too expensive. This is interesting as the German Football League has some of the lowest prices in Europe.

Customers' preferences and how they like to enjoy the game are worthy of analysis. Certainly when looking at the debate between the DFB and the fans, attention has to be paid to the fans as they are vital to the football club's survival. As Merkel points out, when fans are mistreated and not consulted in decisions, they will come together and stand up against what they see as a deceiving move (2012). In his article he reports that the change in timing of TV programming angered the fans as it broke their tradition and routine. If the German Football Federation wants to make any changes it has to look at the preferences of their customers to avoid any type of backlash.

As the survey shows, customers make their choices based on how they want to experience the game and since the Football Federation has so far tried to include its fans in the decision making (Brown and Walsh 2000), it cannot stop now . Atmosphere is not only produced in the standing areas, it is also a major reason why the fans go to the stadiums. Brick points out that implementing seating areas can create a safer environment; however, it also curbs emotions which are hard to simply recreate (2000). Establishing a stadium environment that is overly planned with a fake atmosphere is not the solution.

## 4.4 The public debate on fan behaviour

Fan behaviour issues have been documented in the media over recent years with the debate on what to do reaching the government level. The German Football Federation, the fans, the consumers and the government all have views which do not necessarily match. According to Interior Minister Jäger, some fan groups are made up of different backgrounds such as Nazis, Ultra fans and Hooligans (Stoldt 2013). They have a similar intent to become violent and cause harm either towards other fans or towards the police. However, violence does not only occur in the top Leagues. It also happens in the lower divisions especially on the football field, where players are attacked and referees beaten with police having to come to break up the fights (Bertholz 2013). Because of these incidents there has been discussion that standing room areas have to be removed in football stadiums in order to provide a safer environment (psk 2012).

Figure 4.2 below shows how many people have heard about these discussions either in the media or through friends. Out of the 31 per cent who have not heard about the debate, sixteen per cent were non-football fans and occasional fans, and of the 63 per cent who have heard about it in the media, fifty per cent were football fans. The media focus on this issue has reached mainly the football fans, but there are still some respondents from both sides who are not aware of it at all.

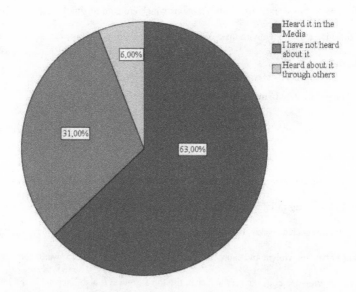

**Figure 4.2 Percentage of respondents who have heard about the debate between the DFB and the Fans concerning the removal of standing room areas**

30

**4.5 Opinion on Fan Behaviour in Stadiums**

Out of the 99 per cent who gave an opinion on what they think is currently happening in German stadiums, 41 per cent described the atmosphere in a negative way showing their disagreement with the situation. However, it is interesting to note that 43 per cent described the fan behaviour in a positive way, not being overly concerned with the problems amongst fans which are currently happening.

Researching the negative responses is interesting as it shows the current perception and image of the fans in Germany. The 41 per cent who described the fan behaviour in a negative manner thought that the way fans behave is ruining football. Respondents to the open-ended questions gave insight into their feelings on fan behaviour. They believe that it is "horrible, violent and disgraceful" and disagree with the use of pyrotechnics. The use of pyrotechnics "destroys the atmosphere and scares the visitors in the stadium." An interesting report comes from a fan who describes, "When pyrotechnics are used, it can happen that one cannot see anything in your block for a period of time which is an added danger." The point is made that fans behave anti-socially and that such aggression and vandalism should not be tolerated inside the stadium or out. Two respondents go as far as relating this type of behaviour to "poor upbringing and poor social skills".

Respondents credit fan disruptions to Ultra fan groups and Hooligans. They believe that these groups are not real fans but are rather out looking for trouble and fights and that the sport has become a secondary issue. "The Ultras are not only destroying the atmosphere but also the image of football." One respondent explains, "It is not about football anymore but more about the rivalry between the fan clubs." Another respondent believes that safety of the fans should be the top priority and that "violent and aggressive fans have no business in the stadium."

A respondent makes an interesting point when he describes the atmosphere of a second division club and how there have always been problems with hooligans which have ruined the experience for the regular fans. He fears for future generations of football fans as he watches the teenagers walking through the streets with a beer in hand on the way to the stadium.

The fan experience is a major factor in game enjoyment and it is interesting to analyse the positive versus the negative sentiment on this issue. The 43 per cent who describe the atmosphere in a positive manner believed that nothing was wrong with the majority of the fans. According to 21 per cent, it was a positive experience but that a small minority ruins it for everyone else and that this small group of people is responsible for the occasional problems which do occur. These respondents believe that the majority of fans, however, do not partake in harmful actions. The stadium experience is a worthy experience, and as a respondent describes "the fan behaviour and atmosphere in Germany is unique in Europe. Ultra fan groups make the experience fascinating because they build the fan culture in the stadiums and create a great atmosphere." He differentiates between the Ultras and the groups who are just there to fight, which should not be allowed. Another respondent who describes himself as a hard-core fan thinks that "fans who support their team 24/7 and the way they choreograph their songs, with jumping up and down and flag waving to support their team, is part of the atmosphere". However, he does stop at racist chants or anti-gay slurs as they cross the line.

Ultras are a major concern for the fans who feel that these groups are the source of the undesired attention. They are modelled on these groups in Italy (Merkel 2007, Kassimeris 2011) where they also have a racist background. These groups have been linked with right wing activity in Germany which is not a new concept in the German Bundesliga (Kassimeris 2009). As Spaaij and Viñas explain, this behaviour originates in the standing areas and has a strong link to national identity (2005). It is interesting to note that while the majority does see fan behaviour in a positive manner, that almost half do recognize that there are troublemakers amongst the fans. As seen in the survey, fans do not enjoy the violent fans and their association with Ultras and Hooligans is to be taken seriously as it influences the fan's view of the game.

The survey revealed an interesting thought process amongst the respondents who compared fan behaviour in Germany to that in other countries. According to eight per cent of the respondents, the atmosphere in German football stadiums is better than in other countries around the world such as in the UK, Italy, Turkey and South America. The respondents are worried that changing anything in Germany will create similar atmospheres as in the UK where they see the atmosphere as stagnant because of the absence of standing room areas. They also think the racism in Italy's League and in the violent derbies in Turkey is worse. Interestingly enough, after violent games in Turkey, the fans are banned from the stadium, and only children and women are allowed into the stadium for the following game. Rivalries can bring forth a hatred towards each other whether it is a different football club or region and therefore games such as derbies can create conflict (Benkwitz and Molnar 2012).

**4.6 Stadium safety**

Figure 4.3 shows the number of respondents who thought that in light of the events happening in the stadiums, something has to change. Despite respondents thinking that something should change, most (66%) feel safe in the stadium. A larger number of respondents do not attend games in a stadium for other reasons than because of concerns for safety. The ten per cent, who do not think something has to change in the stadiums, also do not think that pyrotechnics are dangerous. These numbers are significant as they portray the feeling of safety amongst the fans, yet an understanding that change is necessary.

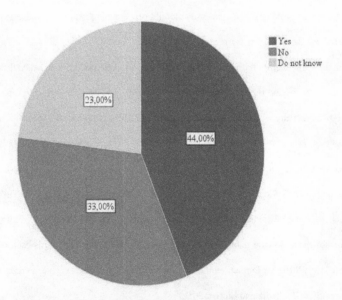

**Figure 4.3 Percentage of respondents who think something has to change in**

**stadiums**

34

Stadiums have meaning for fans as well as for the communities that surround it. There is an attachment that the fan feels towards a stadium and it is a part of a person (Bale 1993). This is in line with the survey as people are still drawn to the stadium. The stadium experience can have an impact on the fan but also an impact on the people living in the surrounding areas which can be negative especially when there is trouble (Bale 2000). Therefore, it is important to make the experience safe and enjoyable for the fans attending matches.

### 4.7 Pyrotechnics in stadiums

As previously explained, Bengalos are used for sea rescue missions and therefore are extremely difficult to extinguish. Despite the known dangers, seventeen per cent of respondents believe that Bengalos are not dangerous. Although 75 per cent do believe that these flares that burn at over a 1000 degrees Centigrade are dangerous, nineteen per cent do not think anything should change in the stadiums.

According to the survey, as seen in Figure 4.6, most of the survey participants believe that pyrotechnics should not be allowed in the stadium. As some respondents answered, having such a flare in a stadium can induce panic amongst people and obstruct the view because of all the smoke. This is in line with the current debate about getting rid of standing room to curb the use of Bengalos because of their dangers and the proposal to create sanctions against people bringing them in. A four year old child was diagnosed with smoke poisoning in a German stadium (express24 2013). A fourteen year old child was killed by a Bengalo as fans threw them into the opposing fan blocks in Bolivia at a football game between a local team and a Brazilian team in a cup match

(Fonseca 2013). The use of pyrotechnics can negatively impact the public's feeling of safety in the stadium and, as the survey results and recent events such as those described above show, stadium attendees are aware of this.

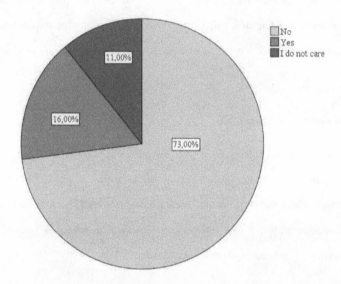

**Figure 4.4 Percentage of respondents who think pyrotechnics should be allowed in stadiums**

As the survey shows, fans are against the use of pyrotechnics. The danger outweighs the appeal that the flares have for the fans especially in such a confined space. Stadiums hold many people in a small space and having any type of panic break out can be dangerous. When a situation grows out of control in such a confined space, even if the cause is not fan related, it can lead to death as was seen in the Hillsborough and Ibrox Stadium disasters (Scraton 2004, Walker 2004). A lack of crowd control can lead to disaster, and fan safety concerns are vital especially dealing with fire (Johnes 2004). As Scraton, Walker and Johnes explain, a stadium setting is a fragile environment where an incident can quickly grow into a major catastrophe and can cause serious injury and death. Therefore, using pyrotechnics in such an environment is a cause for serious concern.

## 4.8 Standing room

Fan atmosphere and culture is created in the standing room areas of German football stadiums. The tickets are cheap, the people sing and wave their flags and choreograph routines to support their team. However, this area is also the area of discussion as officials from the German Football League and the German Football Federation are threatening to get rid of the standing room areas if fan problems do not cease. Other countries have already done this in the English Premier League. The Federal Minister of the Interior, Friedrich, has threatened that similar actions will take place in German stadiums if the violence is not stopped (heb 2012).

Table 4.2 below shows the amount of standing room that exists in each stadium in the first division of the Bundesliga in relation to total capacity of each stadium. As one can see below, this would mean the stadiums would have to remove over 216,000 cheap standing room tickets in the first division alone, which would be 26 per cent of the total capacity.

**Table 4.2 Seating arrangements and total stadium capacity for teams in the first**

**division of the Bundesliga** (transfermarkt 2012)

| Teams | Stadium | Seats | Standing room | Average Attendance | Total Capacity | Location |
|---|---|---|---|---|---|---|
| Hamburger SV | Imtech Arena | 46.500 | 10.500 | 52.500 | 57.000 | Hamburg |
| Eintrach Frankfurt | Commerzbank Arena | 42.200 | 9.300 | 47.404 | 51.500 | Frankfurt |
| FC Bayern Munich | Allianz Arena | 57.343 | 13.794 | 71.000 | 71.137 | Munich |
| VFB Stuttgart | Mercedes Benz Arena | 49.224 | 11.225 | 50.134 | 60.449 | Stuttgart |
| 1.FC Nürnberg | Grundig Stadion | 36.771 | 13.229 | 40.648 | 50.000 | Nürnberg |
| SV Werder Bremen | Weserstadion | 31.200 | 10.900 | 40.483 | 42.100 | Bremen |
| Fortuna Düsseldorf | Esprit Arena | 44.683 | 9.917 | 45.076 | 54.600 | Düsseldorf |
| Hannover 96 | AWD Arena | 41.000 | 8.000 | 43.664 | 49.000 | Hannover |
| FC Augsburg | SGL Arena | 19.160 | 11.500 | 28.904 | 30.660 | Augsburg |
| Borussia Dortmund | Signal Iduna Park | 53.675 | 27.589 | 80.539 | 81.264 | Dortmund |
| SpVgg Greuther Fürth | Trolli Arena | 9.500 | 8.500 | 16.948 | 18.000 | Greuter Fürth |
| FC Schalke 04 | Veltins Arena | 45.364 | 16.309 | 61.104 | 61.673 | Schalke |
| Bayer 04 Leverkusen | Bay Arena | 21.000 | 9.210 | 27.083 | 30.210 | Leverkusen |
| TSG 1899 Hoffenheim | Wirsol Rhein-Neckar-Arena | 21.018 | 9.146 | 25.728 | 30.164 | Hoffenheim |
| Borussia Mönchengladbach | Stadion im Borussia-Park | 37.904 | 16.145 | 48.877 | 54.049 | Mönchengladbach |
| VFL Wolfsburg | Volkswagen Arena | 22.000 | 8.000 | 26.244 | 30.000 | Wolfsburg |
| 1. FSV Mainz 05 | Coface Arena | 20.000 | 13.150 | 30.776 | 33.150 | Mainz |
| SC Freiburg | Mage Solar Stadion | 14.000 | 10.000 | 23.180 | 24.000 | Freiburg |
| | | | | | | |
| Total | | 612.542 | 216.414 | 760.292 | 828.956 | |

As the DFB and the fans discuss the standing room areas, it is clear that fans do not want to lose on this topic. This is in line with the survey as most respondents (69%) think that eliminating standing room areas will have a negative effect. Only eleven per cent saw it positively as it would calm down the fans. One fan describes the result of removing the standing areas, "as the loss of the German fan culture since the stadium atmosphere comes from the standing room".

The German Football Federation believes that the standing room brings out the negative behaviour in the fans. In addition to thinking it would ruin the fan culture, most (62%) respondents think that it will not actually solve the problem and will punish the wrong people. Only eleven per cent of football fans think removing the standing room would have an impact. Having only sitting areas available is not the solution as it would not deter people from standing up during the game. Prices would increase through this change and customers would not be able to afford to go to the games anymore.

The survey results are in line with Nash's view that it would not solve the fan behaviour problems but would just change the demographics of the customer base (Nash 2001). In addition, this could cause disturbances inside the stadium to move outside, thus not getting rid of them (Spaaij 2007). Standing room areas are part of the tradition and a fan describes the removal as "the end to German football".

The DFB thinks that if it removes the standing room it will be able to attract a different type of fan who is not prone to extreme behaviour. The survey results show any change in fan atmosphere would not deter 74 per cent of the respondents from watching the games, although fewer would attend games in the stadium. Out of the 22 per cent who are not sure if they will continue to watch the games, thirteen per cent are football fans of which eleven per cent watch twenty games or more in a season. The survey shows that while the majority do not believe their viewing experience will be impacted by the standing room removal, the hard-core fans are adamant about the negative impact any changes to the stadium will have.

Considering the fan problems in the stadiums and the debate between the Football Federation, the fans and government officials, respondents were asked who has the responsibility to change this climate or whether anything has to be changed. As seen in Figure 4.8, of the respondents who thought that a combination of clubs, fans and football Federation has the responsibility to solve this issue, 48 per cent were football fans. The fans are vested in a combined effort by all parties to find a solution to protect their football.

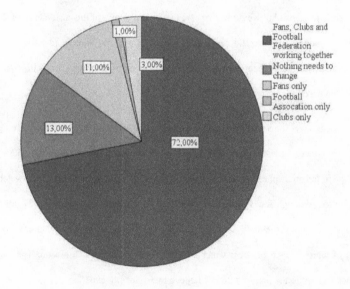

**Figure 4.5 Definition of responsibility for solution to problems with fan behaviour**

**in the stadium as viewed by respondents**

As the survey shows, respondents feel that there is a direct link between the standing areas of the stadium and fan atmosphere. Standing areas and fan groups can be seen as a unifying force for people who come together no matter what their background is to support their team (Batuman 2012). The standing room areas are the heart and soul of the stadium with a special fan culture, which Merkel mentions is preserved in the German Football League (2012). The survey suggests that while fans will continue to watch games, they think removing the standing areas is the wrong approach, and that involving the fans in the solution is vital. As Merkel describes, the Bundesliga is a fan friendly League, and as the survey suggests, embracing the fans is important to continue this type of inclusive fan culture.

**4.9 Respondents' ideas about possible solutions**

If the standing rooms are not removed, then the DFB and the DFL will want to look at other solutions to control some of the extreme behaviour it has seen over recent years. Most respondents (66%) expressed an opinion on how to change the climate in the stadium. Tighter controls at the entrances as well as at the arrival areas such as train stations were the answer, according to fourteen per cent. Respondents expressed the opinion that an open dialogue with fan clubs and members of the clubs' organization was vital to keep this issue under control and as a fan explains, not giving "the disruptive fans the satisfaction of being in the media". Only seven per cent thought the correct approach is preventing access for selected people to stadiums and not letting fans in who are prone to disrupting the games. Handing out stadium bans for offenders and installing better video surveillance systems to catch these people, as well as a larger police presence were key points. One interesting idea came from a respondent who thought that "the clubs have to study and analyse the troublemakers and create campaigns focusing directly on these groups to change their behaviour".

In addition to these proposals, a stricter control of alcohol consumption was suggested and as one respondent mentioned "sell proper beer in the stadium so that one does not have to binge drink prior to the game to keep the buzz during the match". Respondents also suggested public identification of trouble makers and recommended getting the club captains, role models and VIPs campaigning against negative fan behaviour and violence. Role models have been used in the past in Germany to promote correct social behaviour (Magdalinski 1999).

A respondent believed that the reasons for the violence and the trouble makers are because of the social background of these fans, which is a theme repeated in respondents' answers. Respondents suggested dividing the fan areas up into smaller sections and controlling the extremist and right wing fans' entry to the games. "Stewards who are members of fan clubs should be used for fan behaviour control during matches".

Finding a common thread that the fans, the clubs and Football Federation can agree on is important. As Holt explains, different parties involved in football have different interests with the majority concerned about the business aspect (Holt 2007). However, the Bundesliga has a unique structure in which fans make up the majority of the membership of the club and thus participate in the decision making process (Dietl and Franck 2007, Wilkesmann and Blutner 2002). Given the results of the survey and the unique character of the German League, it is evident that finding a solution that is in the best interest of all parties involved is vital.

# CHAPTER 5

## CONCLUSION AND RECOMMENDATION

### 5.1 Conclusion

Over the last years the Bundesliga has experienced tremendous growth in terms of revenue and salary (Martin 2005, Frick 2007). In addition, it has gained extra attention through two German teams playing in the Finals of the Champions League in 2013, plus Bayern Munich hiring the most successful coach in Football, Pep Guardiola. This extra attention has opened the door for the League to showcase its business methods. German football clubs have paid more attention to financial structure and have tried to implement a sustainable method and avoid economic pitfalls which Lago et al. relate to financial problems (Lago et al. 2006). With youth academies, democratic membership structures and inclusive fan culture, the Bundesliga has become a sustainable League.

By creating this successful product, the German Bundesliga has been able to catch up to the other big Leagues such as La Liga in Spain or the English Premier League. The other leagues thrive on international exposure and commercialization and if the Bundesliga wants to move to the top, it must follow suit. In order for the Bundesliga to sell themselves as a unique League, it has to hold on to one of its biggest assets, which is its fan culture. This includes not only the membership structure as explained in Chapter 2.8 but also the standing room areas in the stadium, the fan atmosphere and the cheap ticket prices.

This study shows that the atmosphere is important to the fans and that it draws them to the stadium to watch a game. The survey results underline the link between the atmosphere and the standing room areas, where the life of the stadium is and where fans feel they can show their enthusiasm and excitement. It is part of the culture and tradition and makes the stadium experience so unique. They value this type of atmosphere and are worried a change will create a stale environment.

The study focuses on the importance of safety to the stadium attendees. The respondents attribute the extremely negative behaviour to a minority of the fans. This type of behaviour and use of pyrotechnics can create an unnecessary danger to the rest of the game's attendants. Respondents agree that Bengalos and pyrotechnics should not be allowed and that using them in such a small space is too risky. If something does go wrong, it can quickly escalate and cause injury and death, in addition to major damage to the image of the Bundesliga as a business. Therefore, safety has to be enforced in order for the stadium experience to be an enjoyable one and for the fan culture to continue to flourish.

Respondents thought that removing the standing room which they consider an integral part of the stadium experience is the wrong way to move forward. While fans currently feel safe, they do recognize that actions have to be taken to improve the overall situation. The DFL has to ensure that its fan culture is not dominated by right wing Ultra fan groups. In addition, the price of tickets would increase if standing areas are removed which would scare off many fans.

The Bundesliga prides itself on including its members and fans in their organization and having them participate in the decision making process. Therefore, the respondents think this tradition of all parties working together should continue in order to circumvent troublemakers causing harm to the sport and to the image of football in Germany.

Interestingly enough, both football and non-football fans have heard about the standing room debate which means it is a topic in the mainstream media which the author of this study has observed as well. The fans do not agree with the way this minority is creating a stir with their actions in the fan sections. The fans are proud of the atmosphere in their stadiums and they want to make sure that the fan traditions and cultures are upheld throughout the future.

Finding a solution to the misbehaviour of fans who decide to disrupt football games is important to make the league a presentable product to the rest of the world. This can have a huge impact on sponsorship and TV money. The reports in the media about violence or games being halted due to the smoke from the Bengalos do not help the image of the Bundesliga. If the league wants to compete with the top leagues such as the English Premier League in terms of international TV coverage, then they certainly have to look at all possible solutions. The survey suggests that keeping the standing areas, involving all parties in finding a solution, getting rid of the pyrotechnics and ensuring fan safety inside and outside of the stadium are the key components of the solution moving forward.

From a business perspective the League will have to take these points seriously to be attractive to its stakeholders and continue its growth. In order for the Bundesliga to sell itself as an international product, it will have to combine their business sense with an energetic yet safe fan culture to become one of the top leagues in the world.

## 5.2 Recommendations

The Bundesliga is scrambling to find a solution to the fan disturbances. This author believes there are several viable options in order to continue on the road of success. One of the recommendations is to have tighter controls both going into the stadium, at access points in the surrounding community and during the games. This was a theme amongst some of the respondents and it would certainly help to control the misbehaviour of the few.

The stewards at the entrance gates should have more authority to body search customers, as is done in airports. Rather than just removing the items which are illegal, those customers who bring in these objects such as Bengalos into the stadiums should be sent to the police immediately who will then take their personal information and hand out an immediate fine. If fans are caught multiple times, then the punishment should escalate to stadium bans. These bans apply nationwide; for first time offenders the ban should be for one year, increasing for every additional offense, with fourth time offenders receiving a lifetime ban. The use of the pyrotechnics in such a space is dangerous and fans know that it is illegal.

Before implementing this plan, the DFB and DFL should publicly advertise this information in all newspapers and media outlets to show that they are taking this issue seriously and will hand out punishments accordingly. The clubs and Football Federation would have to look at how they can control the entry to the stadium if a fan is currently banned. This might be done through video surveillance or customized tickets with the name of each of the customers. The governing organizations should be able to keep track of these customers, as organizations know when unwanted fans are trying to cross the border for international matches and are consequently turned away. A similar method can be used in the stadiums to identify and know of the whereabouts of these fans.

Currently the fans who ignite the Bengalos do so in spite of stewards standing around them. The stewards should note the fan who is burning the Bengalo and remove him from the crowd once the flare has burned out. These fans usually try to hide their face or even switch clothes after they have lit a Bengalo, worried about being identified; however, with stewards present in the area it is possible to identify the violators and remove them. They would then face the same punishment as fans trying to smuggle illegal items into the stadiums. A similar tactic is used in concerts where people are removed from the crowd because of their misconduct. It is possible to do the same in a stadium.

An additional recommendation is to distribute flyers and have demonstrations of the impact of Bengalos on fans in a stadium atmosphere. This author knows that some TV and news stations have shown the effects of pyrotechnics on clothes. However, showing it on a TV channel does not reach everyone, and it can be quickly forgotten. These demonstrations need to be displayed on the way to the stadiums, on the walkways and before entering the stadium. This way fans can see first-hand that it takes only seconds for clothing to start burning with no way to extinguish the Bengalos. This might change the behaviour of the few who do chose to use these flares in stadiums and give them perspective. The fans can have the chance to hand in their Bengalos anonymously before entering the stadium and even receive a small reward for it. In addition, it could put peer pressure on these violators. If the pressure comes from their own ranks, they may think twice about bringing Bengalos the next time.

Another recommendation is to publicly identify those fans who choose to endanger the fans in the stadium. If the clubs, the stewards and police are not able to catch the offenders, the clubs could take out an advertisement in the local newspapers during the week with pictures of the audience asking them to stop. In addition, the clubs and Football Federation could offer a reward for identification of the suspects. This public ridicule and branding of violators as opponents of the beloved football club may make violators rethink their behaviour in and outside of the stadium.

In this debate between the DFB and the fans about standing room and possible solutions to negative fan behaviour, open discussions should be used. Some of the options may have legislative impact which needs to be discussed on government level. A dialogue is not enough; actions need to be taken to avoid any further escalation of fan behaviour which would force extreme measures from the clubs and Football Federation.

## 5.3 Further Research

There are several themes which became evident throughout this research which warrant further research. Several respondents linked the negative behaviour to social backgrounds. This could be an interesting area of study, looking at today's social structure of the Ultra and Hooligan fan groups interested in causing harm or disruptions during the football games as well as what it means to be an Ultra fan. In addition, it would be interesting to hear the perspective of members working in football organizations and their view of fan behaviour, Ultras and Hooligans and comparing the two sides.

The impact of negative fan behaviour on sponsorship is another area worthy of research. Are there are any clauses in the sponsorship agreement which deal with this issue? It would be harmful if a particular stadium with a sponsor's name is linked to negative headlines due to fans, or if fans are seen in front of sponsor billboards behaving in a detrimental manner. It would be interesting to know if sponsors have any type of power when it comes to this issue or if their decision making process is impacted by fan behaviour, either in a positive or negative way.

Another area for further investigation is the commercial appeal of pyrotechnics to football fans. Using Google to research Bengalos and pyrotechnics results in a number of sites offering these items for purchase as well as sites campaigning for legalization of use in stadiums in Germany! These campaigns are becoming quite vehement, making it into the media on a regular basis. It would be interesting to research the inability to block the purchase of these items over the internet in Germany and in other countries where Bengalos in stadiums are illegal.

**5.4 Limitations**

The difficulty of this study was the time constraint and resources. It would have been of interest to do a study during the entire season and to contact all football clubs' fan clubs to obtain their opinions on this subject. The study focuses on a sample of 100 German football and non-football fans during the months of May and June 2013, which nevertheless gives us an interesting indication of fan's opinions on this controversial topic. There was also a constraint in the amount of literature available on this topic because the debate is new, and many of the sources come from media accounts rather than literature. This was also part of the appeal to this author as the topic has not yet been researched and written about extensively.

# REFERENCES

Bale, J. (1993) *Sport, Space and the City*, London, UK: Routledge.

Bale, J. (2000) 'The changing face of football: Stadiums and communities', *Soccer& Society*, 1(1), 91-101.

Batuman, E. (2012) 'The view from the stands: life among Istanbul's soccer fanatics', *Soccer& Society*, 13(5-6), 687-700.

Benkwitz, A. and Molnar, G. (2012) 'Interpreting and exploring football fan rivalries: an overview', *Soccer & Society*, 13(4), 479- 494.

Bertholz, D. (2013) 'Das Maerchen vom Guten Spiel', *Stern*, 6.6.2013, 48-56.

Bewarder, M. and Lutz, M. (2013) '"Mit Sieg oder Niederlage hat es nichts mehr zu tun"', available: http://www.welt.de/politik/deutschland/article116394620/Mit-Sieg-oder-Niederlage-hat-es-nichts-mehr-zu-tun.html [accessed 30.5.2013].

Brick, C. (2000) 'Taking offence: Modern moralities and the perception of the football fan', *Soccer & Society*, 1(1), 158-172.

Bromberger, C. (1995) 'Football as world-view and as ritual', *French Cultural Studies*, 6(18), 293-311.

Brown, A. and Walsh, A. (2000) 'Football supporters' relations with their clubs: A European perspective', *Soccer & Society*, 1(3), 88-101.

Conn, D. (2012) 'Far-sighted Germans in a league of their own', *Sunday Independent*, 2.12.2012, 5.

Conn, D. (2013) 'Burgeoning Bundesliga shows Premier League the way', available: http://www.guardian.co.uk/football/blog/2013/may/22/bundesliga-premier-league-champions-league [accessed 25.6.2013].

Dietl, H. M. and Franck, E. (2007) 'Governance Failure and Financial Crisis in German Football', *Journal of Sports Economics*, 8(6), 662-669.

Dobbert, S. (2012) 'Kinder im Fußballstadion Böller, Kakao, Dosenbier', available: http://www.zeit.de/sport/2012-11/bundesliga-stadion-hannover-freiburg-kinder-block-familien-fans [accessed 6.5.2013].

dr/jr (2013) 'Bundesliga breaks 2 billion euro mark in revenue', available: http://www.dw.de/bundesliga-breaks-2-billion-euro-mark-in-revenue/a-16545937 [accessed 23.5.2013].

Elliott, M. and Williams, D. (2001) 'Paradoxes of qualitative research', *Counselling and Psychotherapy Research: Linking research with practice*, 1(3), 181-183.

ESPN (2013) 'Bundesliga Chief calls out at UEFA', available: http://espnfc.com/news/story/_/id/1457455/bundesliga-chief-calls-uefa-spread-profits?cc=5739 [accessed 23.5.2013].

Evans, J. R. and Mathur, A. (2005) 'The value of online surveys', *Internet Research*, 15(2), 195-219.

Evans, R. and Rowe, M. (2002) 'For Club and Country: Taking Football Disorder Abroad', *Soccer & Society*, 3(1), 37-53.

express24 (2013) 'Polizei ermittelt Kind (4) durch Fortuna-Bengalos verletzt', available: http://www.express.de/fortuna-duesseldorf/polizei-ermittelt-kind--4--durch-fortuna-bengalos-verletzt,3292,22319418.html [accessed 18.6.2013].

Fonseca, P. (2013) 'Young fan killed at Corinthians' match after flare thrown from the crowd', available: http://www.dailymail.co.uk/sport/football/article-2282468/A-young-fan-killed-Corinthians-match-flare-thrown-crowd.html [accessed 16.6.2013].

Frick, B. (2007) 'THE FOOTBALL PLAYERS' LABOR MARKET: EMPIRICAL EVIDENCE FROM THE MAJOR EUROPEAN LEAGUES', *Scottish Journal of Political Economy*, 54(3).

Frick, B. (2009) 'Globalization and Factor Mobility The Impact of the "Bosman-Ruling" on Player Migration in Professional Soccer', *Journal of Sports Economics*, 10(1), 88-106.

Frick, B. and Prinz, J. (2006) 'Crisis? What Crisis? Football in Germany', *Journal of Sports Economics*, 7(1), 60-75.

Fritz, O. (2012) 'Gewalt im Fußball Bengalo – was ist das?', available: http://www.dw.de/bengalo-was-ist-das/a-15964324 [accessed 24.5.2012].

Granello, D. H. and Wheaton, J. E. (2004) 'Online Data Collection: Strategies for Research', *Journal of Counseling & Development,* 82(4), 387-393.


heb (2012) 'Gewalt in Fußballstadien: Friedrich droht mit Abschaffung der Stehplätze', available: http://www.spiegel.de/politik/deutschland/friedrich-droht-mit-abschaffung-der-stehplaetze-in-fussballstadien-a-836129.html [accessed 19.6.2013].


Herbert, I. (2012) 'Uefa's Financial Fair Play rules for the Championship put on hold', available: http://www.independent.co.uk/sport/football/football-league/uefas-financial-fair-play-rules-for-the-championship-put-on-hold-7619284.html [accessed 25.6.2013].


Holt, M. (2007) 'The Ownership and Control of Elite Club Competition in European Football', *Soccer & Society,* 8(1), 50- 67.


Hughes, R. (2013) 'Nelson Mandela Grasped the Power of Sports', available: http://www.nytimes.com/2013/06/12/sports/soccer/12iht-soccer12.html?pagewanted=all&_r=0 [accessed 12.6.2013].


Hunt, S. D., Sparkman, R. D., Jr. and Wilcox, J. B. (1982) 'The Pretest in Survey Research: Issues and Preliminary Findings', *Journal of Marketing Research,* 19(2), 269-273.


John, U. and Luetticke, F. (2012) 'Alle 16 Anträge abgesegnet', *Frankfurter Neue Presse,* 13.12.2013, 10.


Johnes, M. (2004) '1 'Heads in the Sand': Football, Politics and Crowd Disasters in Twentieth-Century Britain', *Soccer & Society,* 5(2), 134-151.


Kassimeris, C. (2009) 'Deutschland über Alles: discrimination in German football', *Soccer & Society,* 10(6), 754- 765.


Kassimeris, C. (2011) 'Fascism, separatism and the ultràs: discrimination in Italian football', *Soccer & Society,* 12(5), 677-688.


King, A. (2000) 'Football fandom and post-national identity in the New Europe', *British Journal of Sociology,* 51(3), 419-442.


Lago, U., Simmons, R. and Szymanski, S. (2006) 'The Financial Crisis in European Football : An Introduction', *Journal of Sports Economics,* 7(3), 3-12.

Liew, J. (2013) 'German football has learnt from past mistakes to become football's new superpower',available:http://www.telegraph.co.uk/sport/football/competitions/bunde sliga/10019558/German-football-has-learnt-from-past-mistakes-to-become-footballs-new-superpower.html [accessed 23.5.2013].

Magdalinski, T. (1999) 'Sports history and East German national identity', *Peace Review: A Journal of Social Justice*, 11(4), 539-545.

Martin, P. (2005) 'THE 'EUROPEANIZATION' OF ELITE FOOTBALL', *Soccer & Society*, 7(2), 349-368.

McGowan, T. (2013) 'UEFA wants 10-match bans for racist abuse', available: http://edition.cnn.com/2013/04/10/sport/football/uefa-racism-bans/index.html?iref=allsearch [accessed 24.5.2013].

Merkel, U. (2007) 'Milestones in the Development of Football Fandom in Germany: Global Impacts on Local Contests', *Soccer & Society*, 8(2-3), 221- 239.

Merkel, U. (2012) 'Football fans and clubs in Germany: conflicts, crises and compromises', *Soccer & Society*, 13(3), 359- 376.

Nash, R. (2001) 'English Football Fan Groups in the 1990s: Class, Representation and Fan Power', *Soccer & Society*, 2(1), 39-58.

Pegelow, L. (2012) 'HSV verschärft Kampf gegen Pyrotechnik', available: http://www.welt.de/regionales/hamburg/article106388429/HSV-verschaerft-Kampf-gegen-Pyrotechnik.html [accessed 30.5.2013].

psk (2012) 'Stadion-Sicherheitsdebatte: Fans drohen mit Boykott, DFL bessert nach', available: http://www.spiegel.de/sport/fussball/die-dfl-hat-ihr-sicherheitskonzept-ueberarbeitet-a-867455.html [accessed 17.6.2013].

RPO (2012) 'Polizei warnt: So gefährlich sind "Bengalos"', available: http://www.rp-online.de/niederrhein-nord/duisburg/nachrichten/polizei-warnt-so-gefaehrlich-sind-bengalos-1.2769756 [accessed 24.5.2013].

Ruf, C. (2012) 'Bengalo-Randale: Stinkefinger von den Hardcore-Ultras', available: http://www.spiegel.de/sport/fussball/relegation-fortuna-gegen-hertha-wird-zum-skandalspiel-a-833553.html [accessed 25.6.2013].

Schöbel, S. (2011) 'Kosten für Polizeieinsätze beim Fußball: Streit im uniformierten Block', available:http://www.n-tv.de/politik/Streit-im-uniformierten-Blockarticle3634876.html [accessed 30.5.2013].

Scraton, P. (2004) '4 Death on the Terraces: The Contexts and Injustices of the 1989 Hillsborough Disaster', *Soccer & Society*, 5(2), 183- 200.

Shergold, A. (2013) '£104 - the bargain price of a Bayern Munich season ticket... and German chief explains why it puts rip-off Premier League to shame', available: http://www.dailymail.co.uk/sport/football/article-2318209/Bayern-Munich-season-tickets-low-104-putting-Premier-League-shame.html [accessed 24.5.2013].

Spaaij, R. (2007) 'Football Hooliganism in the Netherlands: Patterns of Continuity and Change', *Soccer & Society*, 8(2-3), 316-334.

Spaaij, R. and Viñas, C. (2005) 'Passion, politics and violence: A socio-historical analysis of Spanish ultras', *Soccer & Society*, 6(1), 79- 96.

Stoldt, T.-R. (2013) 'Erobern Nazis die Stadien?', available: http://www.welt.de/regionales/duesseldorf/article113301731/Erobern-Nazis-die-Stadien.html [accessed 16.6.2013].

Theuri, P. M. and Turner, L. D. (2002) 'Conducting Survey Research Through an Enhanced Online Web Survey Procedure', *Journal of Internet Commerce*, 1(4), 37-53.

transfermarkt (2012) 'The stadiums of the 1.Bundesliga', [online], available: http://www.transfermarkt.com/en/1-bundesliga/stadien/wettbewerb_L1.html [accessed

Van Selm, M. and Jankowski, N. W. (2006) 'Conducting Online Surveys', *Quality & Quantity*, 40(3), 435-456.

Walker, G. (2004) '3 'The Ibrox Stadium Disaster of 1971'', *Soccer & Society*, 5(2), 169-182.

Wallrodt, L. (2012) 'Der Fußball bekommt die Gewalt nicht in den Griff', available: http://www.welt.de/sport/fussball/article13906644/Der-Fussball-bekommt-die-Gewalt-nicht-in-den-Griff.html [accessed 30.5.2013].

Wilkesmann , U. and Blutner, D. (2002) 'Going Public: The Organizational Restructuring of German Football Clubs', *Soccer & Society,* 3(2), 19-37.


Zeus     (2013)     'Diskussion     über     Bengalos',     available: http://www.derwesten.de/zeusmedienwelten/zeus/fuer-schueler/zeus-regional/dinslaken/diskussion-ueber-bengalos-id7988191.html [accessed 28.5.2013].

# APPENDICES

## Appendix A

### Survey in German

**Seite 1**

1. Geschlecht *
   ○ Männlich
   ○ Weiblich

2. Alter *
   ○ < 18
   ○ 18-24
   ○ 25-35
   ○ 35-50
   ○ 50+

3. Bist du ein Fußballfan? *
   ○ Ja
   ○ Nein
   ○ Nicht wirklich aber ich schaue Spiele gelegentlich an

4. Wie oft schaust du Fußball in der Saison? *
   ○ 0
   ○ 1-6
   ○ 7-13
   ○ 14-20
   ○ 20+

5. Bist du Mitglied eines Fanklubs? *
   ○ ja
   ○ nein

6. Wie oft gehst du ins Stadion in der Saison? *
   ○ 0
   ○ 1-4
   ○ 5-10
   ○ 11-17
   ○ 17+

**Seite 2**

7. Würdest du mit deiner Familie, Kinder, Enkelkindern ins Stadion gehen? *
   ○ ja
   ○ nein

8. Würdest du lieber sitzen oder stehen, wenn du ins Stadion gehen würdest? *
   ○ Stehen
   ○ Sitzen
   ○ Beides

9. Warum ? (Bezieht sich auf Frage 8 )

10. Von wo schaust du am liebsten Fußball Spiele? *
    ○ Im Stadion
    ○ Schaue kein Fußball
    ○ Zuhause
    ○ Bei Freunden
    ○ Bar/ Restaurant

11. Warum? (Bezieht sich auf Frage 10)

**Seite 3**

12. Hast du über die Debatte zwischen dem DFB und den Fans wegen der Eliminierung

der Stehplätze *

○　In den Medien gehört

○　Durch andere erfahren

○　Ich habe davon noch nicht gehört

13. Was denkst du von dem Fan Verhalten in Deutschen Stadien? *

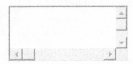

14. Denkst du, es muss sich etwas ändern in den Stadien? *

○　Ja

○　Nein

○　Weiß ich nicht

15. Fühlst du dich sicher im Stadion? *

○　ja

○　nein

○　Gehe nicht ins Stadion

16. Findest du Pyrotechnik im Stadion gefährlich? *

○　Ja

○　Nein

○　Keine Meinung

17. Denkst du Pyrotechnik sollte im Stadion erlaubt sein? *

○ Ja

○ Nein

○ Ist mir egal

**Seite 4**

18. Was denkst du über die DFB Idee die Stehplätze abzuschaffen? *

19. Würdest du ins Stadion gehen, wenn die Stehplätze abgeschafft werden? *

○ Ja

○ Nein

○ Gehe nicht ins Stadion

20. Würde die Abschaffung der Stehplätze die Situation in den Fanblocks lösen? *

○ Ja

○ Nein

○ Weiss ich nicht

21. Wer hat die Verantwortung das Klima im Stadion zu ändern, Fans, Klubs, Fußball Bund oder alle? *

○ Fans

○ Klubs

○ Fußball Bund

○ Alle drei zusammen

○ Denke nicht das es was zu ändern gibt

22. Wie kann man das Klima im Stadion verbessern?

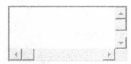

23. Würdest du weiterhin Fußball schauen, wenn die Fan Atmosphäre sich ändert? *

○ Ja

○ Nein

○ Weiß ich nicht

Survey in English

**Page 1**

1. Gender *
   - ○ Male
   - ○ Female

2. Age *
   - ○ < 18
   - ○ 18-24
   - ○ 25-35
   - ○ 35-50
   - ○ 50+

3. Are you a football fan? *
   - ○ Yes
   - ○ No
   - ○ I occasionally watch games

4. How often do you watch games in a season? *
   - ○ 0
   - ○ 1-6
   - ○ 7-13
   - ○ 14-20
   - ○ 20+

5. Are you a member of a fan club? *
   - ○ Yes
   - ○ No

6. How often do you go to the stadium in a season? *

○  0

○  1-4

○  5-10

○  11-17

○  17+

**Page 2**

7. Would you go to the stadium with your family, your kids or grandkids? *

○  Yes

○  No

8. If you were to go to the stadium would you rather sit or stand? *

○  Stand

○  Sit

○  Both

9. Why? (Relates to question 8 )

```
[                    ]
```

10. Where do you prefer to watch football games? *

○  In the stadium

○  Do not watch football

○  At home

○  At friends

○  Bar/ Restaurant

11. Why? (Relates to question 10)

**Page 3**

12. Have you heard about the debate between the DFB and the Fans about the removal

of standing room areas *

- ○ Yes in the media
- ○ Yes through others
- ○ I have not heard about it

13. What do you think about the fan behaviour in German stadiums? *

14. Do you think something has to change in the stadiums? *
- ○ Yes
- ○ No
- ○ I do not know

15. Do you feel safe in the stadiums *
- ○ Yes
- ○ No
- ○ Do not go to the stadiums

16. Do you think pyrotechnics is dangerous? *

○ Yes

○ No

○ No opinion

17. Do you think pyrotechnics should be allowed in stadiums? *

○ Yes

○ No

○ I do not care

**Page 4**

18. What do you think about the idea by the DFB to remove standing room areas? *

19. Would you go to the stadiums if standing room areas were removed? *

○ Yes

○ No

○ Do not go to the stadiums

20. Would the removal of the standing rooms get rid of the problems in the fan areas? *

○ Yes

○ No

○ I do not know

21. Who has the responsibility to change the climate in the stadiums, fans, clubs, football association or all three? *

○ Fans
○ Clubs
○ Football association
○ All three
○ Do not think anything needs to be changed


22. How can one improve the climate in the stadium?

[text box]


23. Would you continue to watch football if the fan atmosphere changed? *

○ Yes
○ No
○ I do not know

Appendix C

Information Sheet (German)

## 1. Einführung

Mein Name ist Herr Pascal Adams. Ich bin ein Student in dem Center für Sports Studies in der Schule für Public Health, Physiotherapy and Population Science an der University College Dublin. Ich lade dich ein an diesem Forschungsprojekt teilzunehmen. Diese Studie nimmt Bezug auf das Verhalten der Fans in deutschen Fußball Stadien und über den Vorschlag Stehplätze aus den Stadien zu entfernen. Ich bin interessiert an der Meinung von den Seiten des Fußballfans sowie der allgemeinen Öffentlichkeit.

## 2. Worüber ist diese Forschung?

Diese Studie bezieht sich auf die Fan Atmosphäre in deutschen Fußball Stadien und über die Debatte Stehplätze aus den Stadien zu entfernen.

## 3. Warum studiere ich dieses Thema?

Diese Studie ist Teil eines MSc in Sport and Excercise Management Abschluss an der University College Dublin.

## 4. Warum wurdest du ausgewählt?

Du wurdest ausgewählt, weil ich an deiner Meinung über dieses Thema interessiert bin. Ich bin daran interessiert zu lernen, ob du denkst, dass es momentan Probleme gibt in den Stadien oder ob es einfach ein Teil der Atmosphäre ist und dazugehört. Wenn du einverstanden bist, kannst du den Fragebogen ausfüllen, der nur ein paar Minuten dauert.

**5. Wie werden die Daten benutzt?**

Die Information wird benutzt, um zu sehen, welcher Meinung Fußball Fans und die allgemeine Öffentlichkeit über die Situation in den Fußball Stadien denkt.

**6. Wie wird deine Privatsphäre geschützt?**

Es wird keine identifizierbare Information in dem Fragebogen von dir gespeichert. Das heißt, dass niemand weiß, welche Fragen du beantwortet hast und was deine Antworten waren. Da es anonym ist, kannst du leider nachdem du die Fragen beantwortet hast nicht wieder zurück nehmen, da niemand weiß, welche Antworten deine waren.

**7. Was sind die Risiken oder Vorteil für die Teilnahme an dieser Studie?**

Es gibt keine bekannten Risiken oder Vorteile, wenn man an dieser Studie teilnimmt.

**8. Kann ich meine Meinung ändern und nicht an der Studie teilnehmen?**

Deine Teilnahme an dieser Studie ist freiwillig und du kannst jederzeit den Fragebogen vorzeitig beenden, ohne eine Erklärung zu geben.

**9. Wie kann ich die Resultate rausfinden über diese Studie?**

Wenn du die Resultate wissen möchtest, kannst du mich direkt kontaktieren (Kontakt Information weiter unten) oder das Zentrum für UCD Sports Studies anrufen.

**10. Was ist, wenn ich weiter Fragen habe, über dieses Projekt?**

Wenn du an der Studie teilnehmen möchtest, fülle bitte den Fragebogen aus und behalte eine Kopie dieses Informationsblatt für dich. Falls du weiter fragen hast über diese Studie kannst du mich direkt kontaktieren oder das Zentrum für UCD Sports Studies direkt anrufen unter

Vielen Dank für deine Kooperation.

Pascal Adams

MSc Sport and Exercise Management

University College Dublin

## Appendix D

## Information Sheet English

### 1. Introductory Statement

My name is Mr. Pascal Adams. I am a student in the Centre for Sports Studies in the School of Public Health, Physiotherapy and Population Science at University College Dublin. I am inviting you to take part in my research project, Fan Atmosphere in German football stadiums. I will be researching the feeling among the public and the football fans about the changing atmosphere in German football stadiums and the proposal to remove standing room from the venues.

### 2. What is this research about?

The research focuses on the fan atmosphere in German football stadiums and the proposal from the German government to remove standing room areas in the stadiums as a result.

### 3. Why are you doing this research?

This study is being completed as part of the MSc Sport and Exercise Management degree.

### 4. Why have you been chosen?

You have been selected because I am interested in your opinion and your perception of the issue and whether you think it's a serious problem or not. If you agree to participate in this research, you will be asked to take part in the online survey which will only take a few minutes to answer.

**5. How will the data be used?**

The data will be used to analyse the feeling among the football fans as well as the non-football fans about the current issues in German football stadiums.

**6. How will you protect my privacy?**

No identifiable information (such as your name or address) will be collected from you in the questionnaire, which means that no-one will know what responses you have given. However, as the individual questionnaire cannot be linked to you, if you decide to withdraw from the study after you submit your questionnaire, it will not be possible to remove your questionnaire, as there is no way to know which one is yours.

**7. What are the benefits and risks of taking part in this research study?**

There are no known risks to you from taking part in this research, and no foreseeable direct benefits to you. However, it is hoped that the research will benefit the German football league and give the league some information of how the public and the fans feel.

**8. Can I change my mind at any stage and withdraw from the study?**

Your participation in this research is voluntary. You are free to refuse to take part at any time, without giving a reason. You may refuse to answer any questions and may stop taking part in the study at any time without disadvantage.

**9. How will I find out what happens with this project?**

If you would like to know the results of this study, you are free to contact me directly (see contact details below) or the UCD Centre for Sports Studies.

**10. What if I have any further questions about this project?**

If you agree to participate in this study, please fill in the questionnaire and return to me and keep a copy of this information sheet for your future reference. Please take time to consider whether you want to take part in this research or not. If you have any questions about the research, please email me at the contact details provided below or contact the UCD Centre for Sports Studies at

Thank you in advance for your cooperation,

Pascal Adams


MSc Sport and Exercise Management

University College Dublin

CPSIA information can be obtained
at www.ICGtesting.com
Printed in the USA
LVHW090448081122
732583LV00005B/228